Kindergarten Kids

by Ellen B. Senisi

Cartwheel
·B·O·O·K·S·®

SCHOLASTIC INC.

New York Toronto London Auckland Sydney

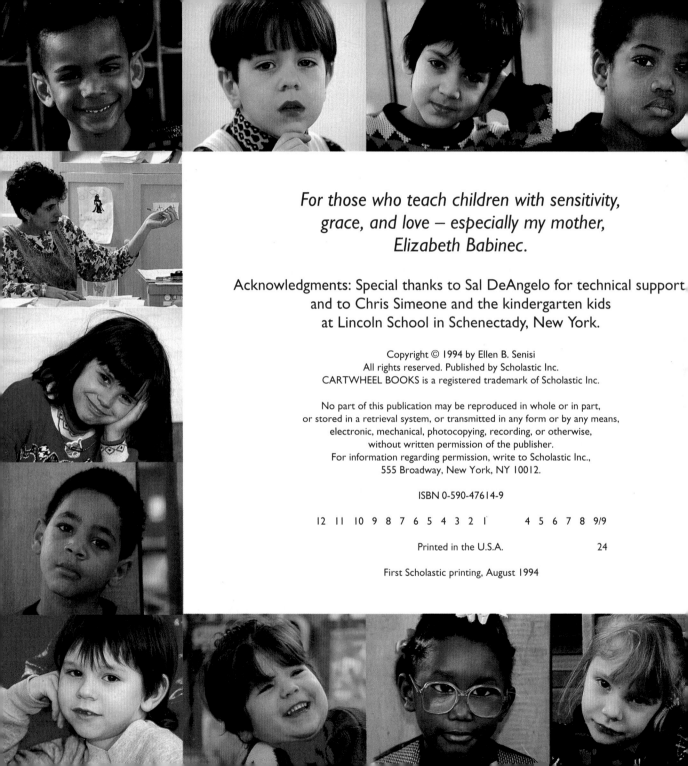

*For those who teach children with sensitivity,
grace, and love – especially my mother,
Elizabeth Babinec.*

Acknowledgments: Special thanks to Sal DeAngelo for technical support,
and to Chris Simeone and the kindergarten kids
at Lincoln School in Schenectady, New York.

ISBN 0-590-47614-9

12 11 10 9 8 7 6 5 4 3 2 1   4 5 6 7 8 9/9

Printed in the U.S.A.   24

First Scholastic printing, August 1994

There are twenty-one kids in Room 8 at Lincoln School. Before they were old enough to come to kindergarten, they used to wonder, *What is it like? Will I have any friends?* Now, they can tell other kids what it's like in *their* kindergarten.

School starts when the bell rings. The kids come into the classroom and say hello to their friends and their teacher, Mrs. Simeone. Mrs. Simeone says good morning to everyone, too.

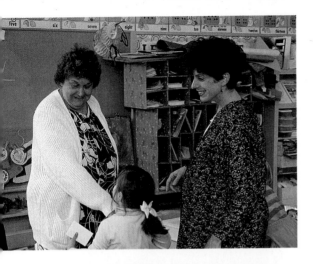

There's a lot to do in kindergarten. The class gets started right away. Kayla says good-bye to her grandma. And Mrs. Simeone says, "Everyone, choose a learning center to work at."

"Mrs. Simeone, I don't know which center to choose!" says Mar'Keith.

"The rice center is out!" says Dominique to Mar'Keith. "That's where *I* want to work." Dominique likes how the rice feels running through his fingers.

Everyone likes to play in the house corner.
"Richard, here's your breakfast," says LaVonne.

Working and playing in the learning centers is Rochelle's favorite part of the day. She might work on the computer with Ahmad. Or she might play mommies in the house corner with Kayla.

Mrs. Simeone is going to be a real mommy. "She's going to have *twins*!" says Marchane.

Mrs. D. is the teacher's helper. She doesn't come every day. But when she does come, everyone is happy to see her. "She always smiles at me," says Michael. "She likes me."

Michael and Meagan like to play with blocks.

"There are many blocks in our room," says Meagan.

There are big blocks and little blocks. Yolanda uses the pattern blocks.

"See what I made, Mrs. Simeone!" says Christina.

Everyone has a favorite center.

Kenny and Richard like playing in the water tub with William, who is visiting today.

Steven says, "Sand is fun to look at and feel."

Brittany loves to dress up and pretend to be someone else.

Suddenly the principal's voice comes over the loudspeaker on the classroom wall, "Will everyone please rise for the Pledge of Allegiance?"

"I love saying the pledge. It makes me feel grown-up," says Shakoa. "When the pledge is over, our teacher says, 'You may continue.' And we start playing again."

After a while, the teacher flicks the lights off and on. That means it's time for everyone to clean up.

"I can put away all these blocks by myself," says Shakoa. "I think clean-up is more fun at school than it is at home."

"Mrs. D., can you help me finish this puzzle?" asks Kayla.

"Uh-oh," says Mrs. Simeone. "I think we need the broom at the sand table.

"After we clean up, we sit together on the rug," says Kenny.

Mrs. Simeone takes out the attendance rds. She calls out names to see who is class. The girls' names are on the pink rds, and the boys' names are on the blue rds.

"I like when it's my turn to be the helper," says Rachel. "I help my teacher put the date on the calendar."

Next the class talks together. Everyone wants to talk at once. But Mrs. Simeone has each child take a turn. "We talk about the things we made the day before," says Brittany. "And the teacher tells us what our work is for the rest of the day."

"My teacher shows me how to [d]o things," says James. "She teaches [u]s letters and all about following [r]ules."

"Mrs. Simeone always makes me [f]eel better when I get hurt," says [L]aVonne.

"I like Mrs. Simeone because she [s]ays funny things," says Jessica.

Then it was time to go outside. It was cold and we walked on a trail with a bridge. When we arrived at a tree with a tap and a bucket we stopped. The bucket was half-filled with sap. It looked like water with ice in it. We all got to taste the sap. It tasted like sugar water. We walked on the trail to an outdoor fire where the sap was boiling into syrup.

Soon Mrs. Simeone gets the class started on their work. Everyone works on coloring projects together.

Meagan works very carefully.

"That looks good, Rochelle," says Scott.

Yolanda finishes coloring very quickly.

Sadaf and Richard color plants and seeds in their coloring book.
Kenny and Brittany color the letter S.

A lot of the classwork is about the alphabet. The kids practice the alphabet many ways. "When we learned the letter Q, I made a queen's crown," says Rac
"We painted with Q-tips, too," says Mar'Keith.
"And we sat around a quilt," says Marchane.

The class practiced writing the letter R by tracing it with red paint.

For the letter S, the class read a book about stone soup — and then they made some! Yolanda helped to wash the stones. "We washed them lots of times until they got clean," she says.

"The soup was good. But we didn't eat the stones," says LaVonne.

After all that work, Marchane is ready to rest. It's a good thing that it's snack time. "Put your papers in your mailboxes," says Mrs. Simeone.

"Before snack time, we go to the bathroom and we wash our hands," says Brittany.

Snack time is a good time to be with friends. "Guess what?" says Shakoa. "I lost a tooth!"

"Do you think your mother will let you come to my house to play?" Ahmad asks Brittany.

Sometimes kids have problems with each other. But Mrs. Simeone does not let any student hurt or tease another student.

"You do 'time out' when you don't follow the rules," says Richard. "That means you sit by yourself. You can't be with the other kids until the teacher says you can."

There's more work to do after snack time. It may be science or math. For one science lesson, everyone planted seeds and took care of them. Soon plants grew from the seeds. "Watch out, Scott," says Sadaf. "That's too much water!"

It's time for math! The class practices counting things. James likes to use the bunny counters.

"We count money, too," says Richard. "Real money!"

On some days, the class does art projects after snack time. "Michael, you're making a wonderful picture," says Mrs. Simeone.

Sometimes everyone works together on a big art project.

"One time, we made our own paper," says Jessica.

"We learn music in kindergarten, too," says Rochelle. "We sing together or make music with rhythm sticks."

Most of the time, school is fun. But sometimes kids get tired. Sometimes they're not sure what to do. And sometimes they just have a bad day.

But if someone has a problem, it's all forgotten when the teacher says, "Line up to go outside!"

On the playground, everyone shouts and laughs. The kindergarten kids jump, run, climb, slide, and swing.

After the class comes back inside, Mrs. Simeone says, "Time to settle down now." Then she reads a story to the class.

"Sometimes we tell stories to each other, too," says LaVonne.